BORIS VALLEJO'S 3D MAGIC®

Images created by Al. E. Barber

Foreword by Boris Vallejo

Stewart, Tabori & Chang
New York

First published by Dragon's World Ltd 1995

© Dragon's World Ltd 1995
© Al. E. Barber 1995
© Original images Boris Vallejo 1995
Al. E. Barber is Arin and Garin O' Aivazia and Gervais Clifton

Published in 1995 and distributed in the U.S. by Stewart, Tabori and Chang,
a division of U.S. Media Holdings, Inc
575 Broadway, New York, N.Y. 10012

ISBN 1-55670-431-3

Library of Congress Catalog Card Number: 95-69586

Printed in Spain

10 9 8 7 6 5 4 3 2 1

FOREWORD BY
BORIS VALLEJO

I have been a professional artist for the past thirty-eight years, more than
twenty of those in the fantasy field. Throughout those years I have seen my
work reproduced in many different forms: books, poster, T-shirts, belt
buckles, jewellery, clocks, skate boards, etc., etc. While I can, reluctantly,
admit to having a somehow narcissistic enjoyment of seeing all these
products around, it is also fair to say that I am reasonably used to seeing my
paintings in print. None of this, however, had prepared me for the impact of
viewing the samples that I received from Dragon's World for this 3-D book.
Even without the three-dimensional effect, the visual quality knocked me off
my socks. Here was a totally new way of looking at my own paintings.
Something fresh and exciting. A bizarre marriage between a very traditional
style of painting and space age technology.

I was born in Lima, Peru. A very traditional city in a country of ancient
history. My artistic studies took place in an art school that not only
encouraged but demanded an academic approach to drawing and painting.
I departed, to a certain extent, from the strict discipline of my training by
becoming an illustrator. A smart move, from my point of view, and one
I have never regretted. Being a traditional artist, I have resisted the concept
of computers for many years. I still do not believe that computers will replace
the artist as some people fear, but now, I see computers as an incredibly
useful tool that can be used to explore new avenues and achieve these unusual
3-D effects.

For you, as you hold this book in your hands right now, I can only say:
'Welcome to the future!'

Boris Vallejo
Spring, 1995

Lavalite World

For the cover of this book of adventures, Boris Vallejo created this visually arresting action scene with the hero and heroine riding a tree trunk into battle.

The translation of the original image into its 3D interpretation can be seen here quite clearly in these two examples.

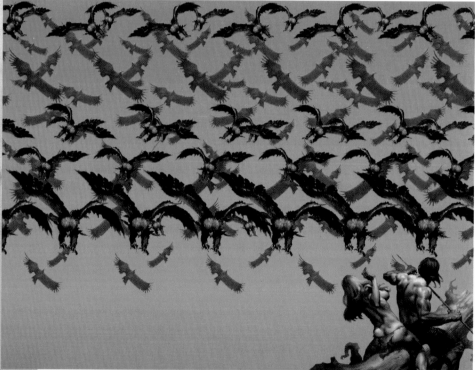

Introduction to
Boris Vallejo in 3D Magic®

Most of the 3D pictures in this book need a *wall-eyed* viewing technique. This means that your eyes must be made to look at a point further away than the picture, whilst your eye-lenses maintain their focus on the surface (see figure 1). Some people can just relax their eyes, by staring blankly through the picture, and access the 3D model hidden within. For those of you who are less lucky or practised, there are two effective methods to achieve the desired eye configuration.

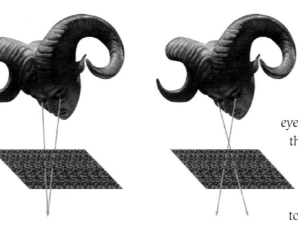

Figure 1   **Figure 2**

image should become clearer. Again it might help to move your head slightly from side to side. Now slowly move your eyes to look around the whole picture. If at any stage you focus on the picture in the normal manner, simply look again at your reflection in the glass

Pictures marked with crossed arrows are designed to be looked at using a *cross-eyed* viewing technique. This means your eyes are directed at a point closer to you than the page, while still being focused on the page (see figure 2). This technique allows us to use bigger pictures on the surface strikingly related to the 3D image hidden within. Unfortunately the 3D pictures inside are neither as easy, nor as relaxing to view. To begin with especially your eyes may get tired trying to see them. If this happens take a break.

Method 1
Hold a picture to the end of your nose, relax, and stare blankly through the page. Everything will appear unfocused. Your eyes will be in their resting position, pointing as if at an object in the far distance. Now *without changing the position of your eyes*, slowly move the book away until it is 18-24 inches from your face. Keep your eyes exactly where they are. Relax. You should be able to see a 3D quality in the page. Keep your eyes directed at a point through the page, while you focus them accurately on the surface, and a sharp 3D image should snap into place. If not, try moving your head from side to side a little, or try moving the book back and forth an inch or two. Now slowly move your eyes to look around the whole picture. If at any stage your eyes flick back to their normal viewing position, start the whole process again by holding the picture to your nose.

Method 2
Place a pane of glass, or similar shiny transparent material over the picture you want to view. Hold them both 18-24 inches from your face. Look at your reflection in the glass. Relax. Again you should see a 3D quality in the surface of the image. Now transfer your attention to the picture, without actually moving your eyes. The 3D

Method 3
Hold the picture about 2 feet from your face. Hold your finger up halfway between your eyes and the book, and focus on it. Lower your finger keeping your eyes in the same place. You should be able to see two translucent images of the picture floating near the middle of your vision, perhaps already partially overlapping. Cross your eyes more or less to overlap the two half-images exactly. Then, keeping your eyes' direction steady, focus on the surface, and watch the amazing 3D version emerge.

You might find it helpful to overlap the two translucent images while you are still holding up your finger. To do this, move your finger closer or further away, focusing on it the whole time. When you can see the two images on the page in the background almost overlapping but still blurred, pull your finger away.

Fusion Dots
At the top of each page you will notice two dots. These are to help you fine tune your eye position when you are trying to view the 3D images. If you can see three focused dots using an appropriate technique for that picture, then your eyes are in exactly the right place to access the 3D shapes below.

It has been claimed that viewing these pictures increases the proportion of alpha brain waves, that are usually associated with deep sleep and meditation, and encourages a greater number of neural connections in your brain's visual centre.

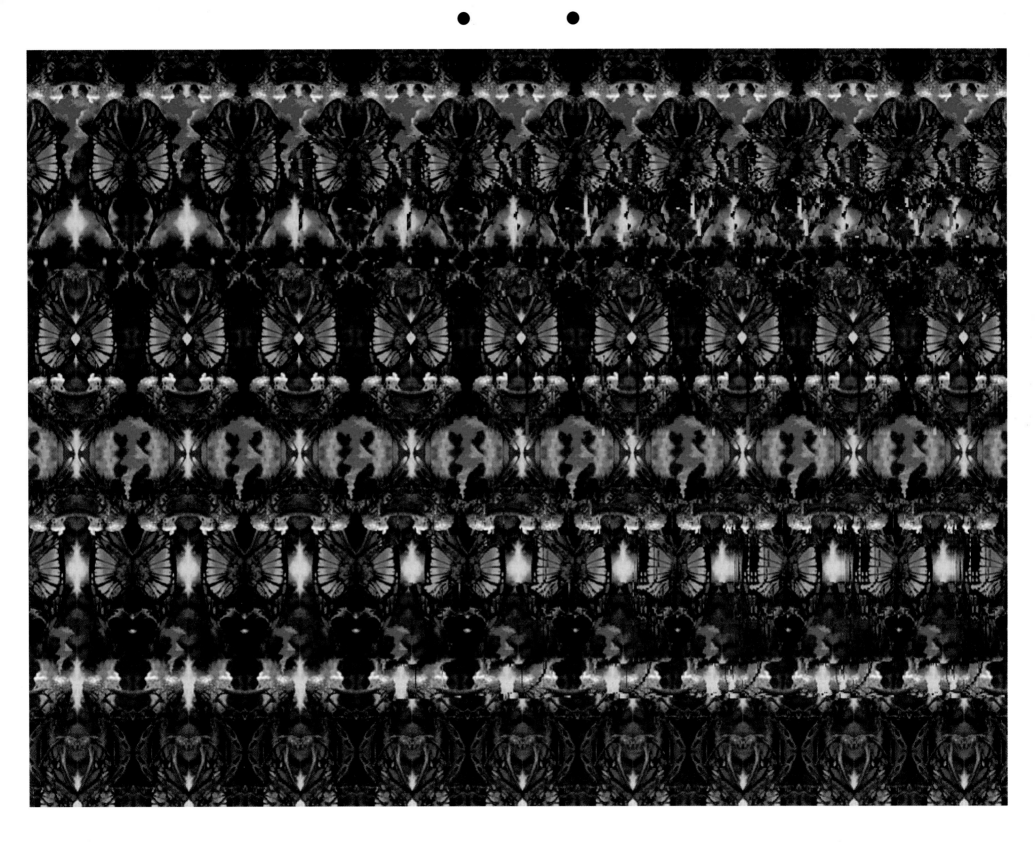

BORIS IN 3D

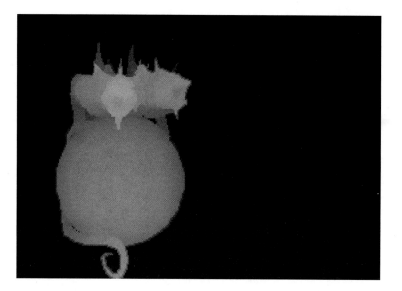

SLAYER

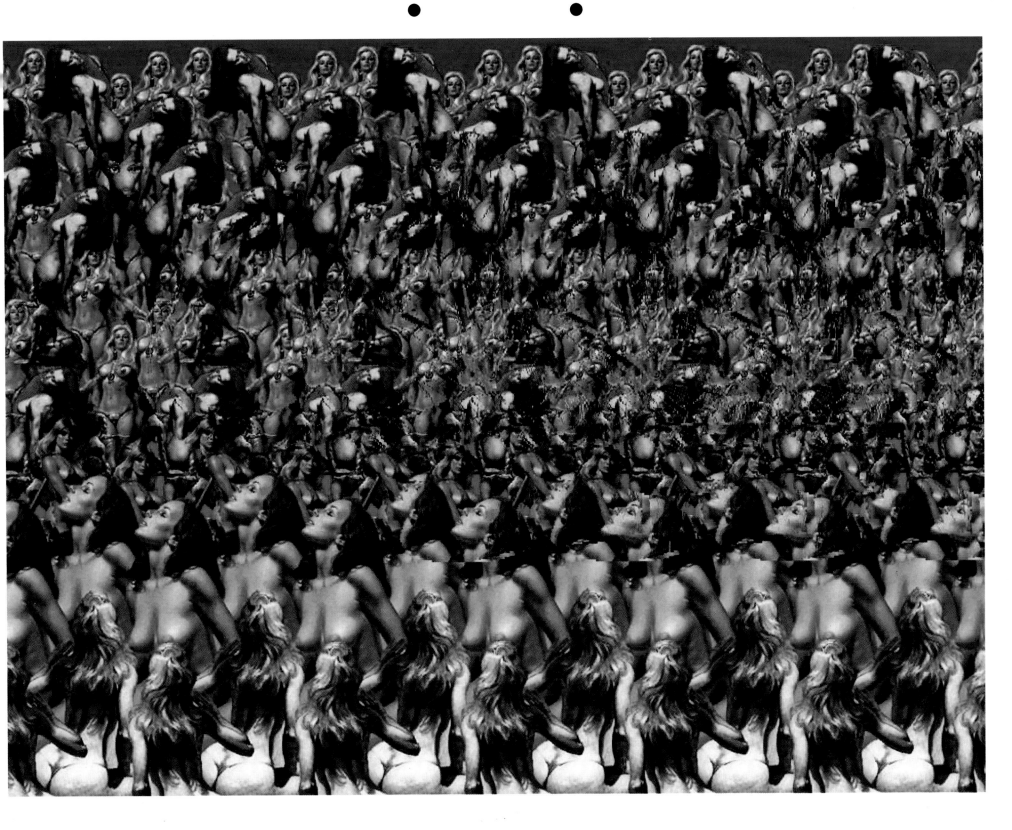

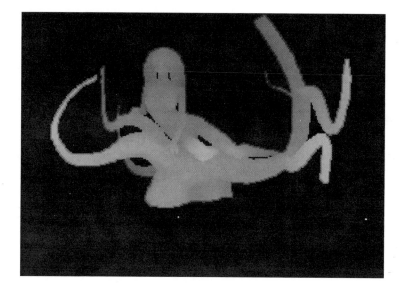

LIONESS

FANTASY FLIGHT

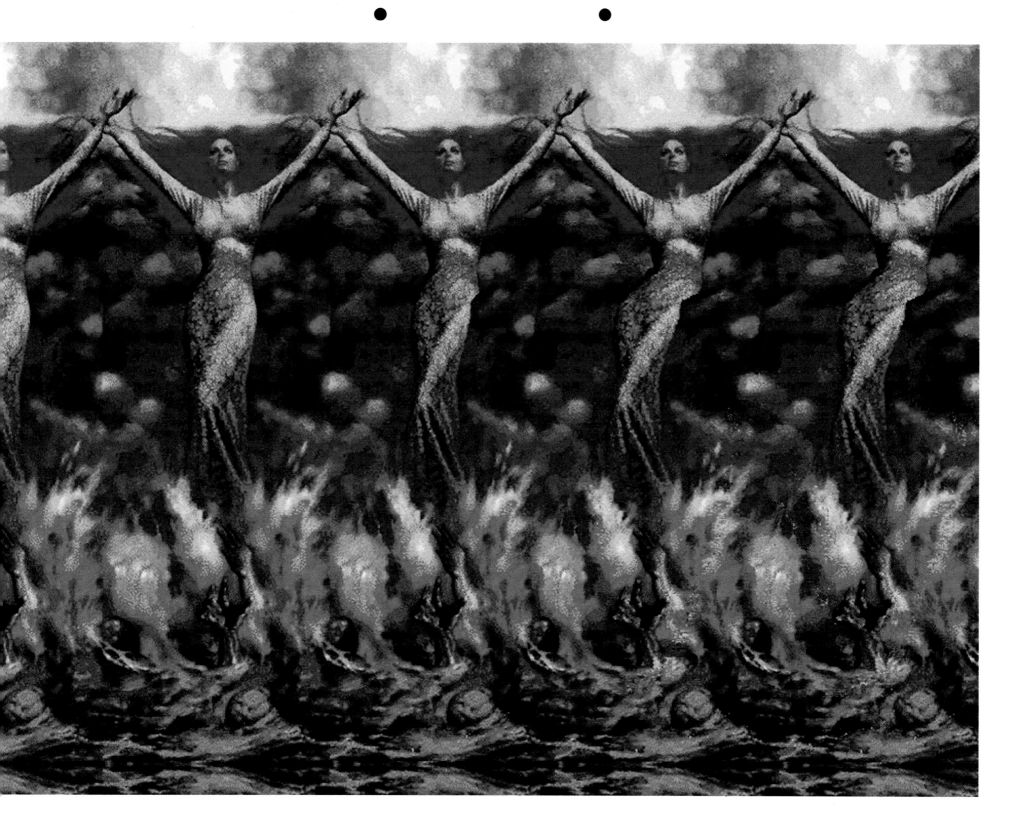

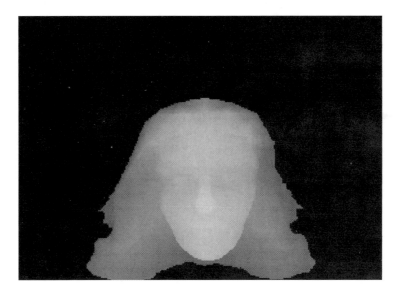

THETIS

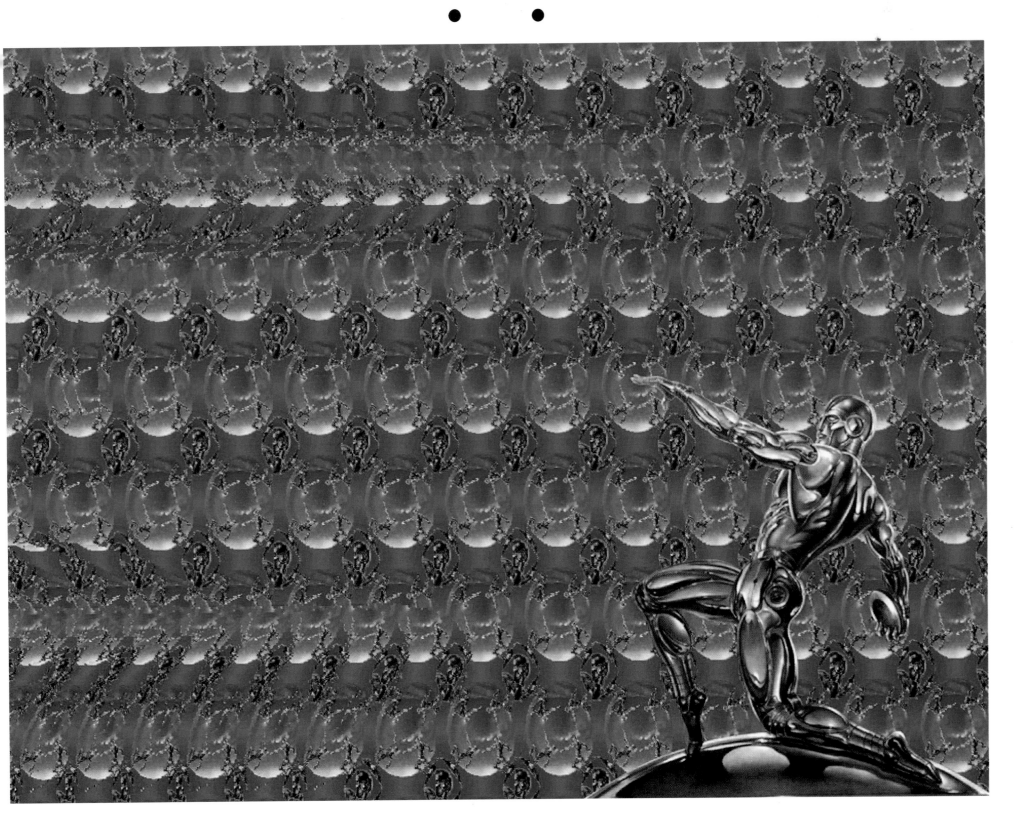

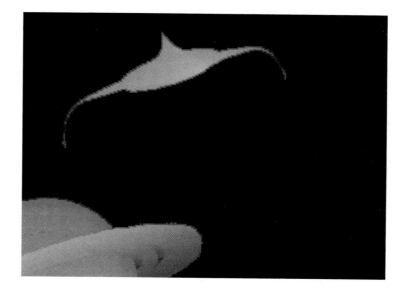

XETAR

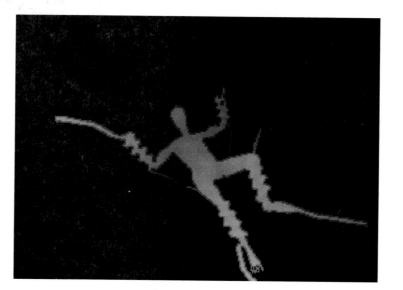

WRITHING

GEMINI

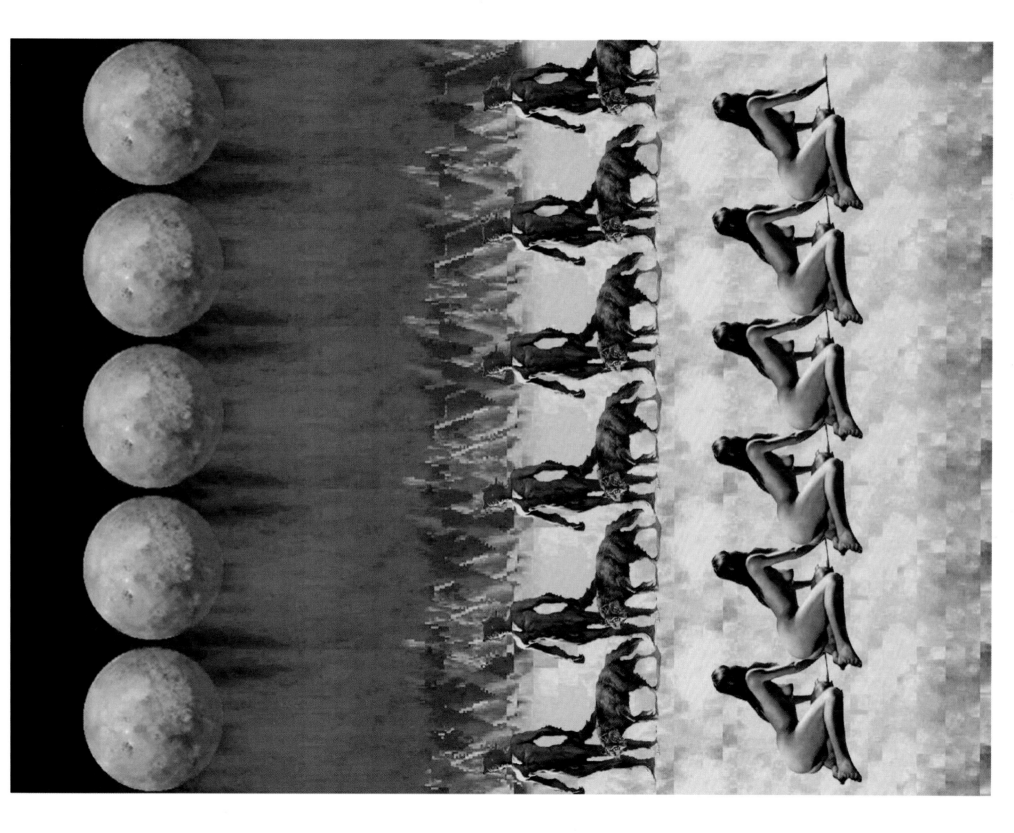

WOLFMAN

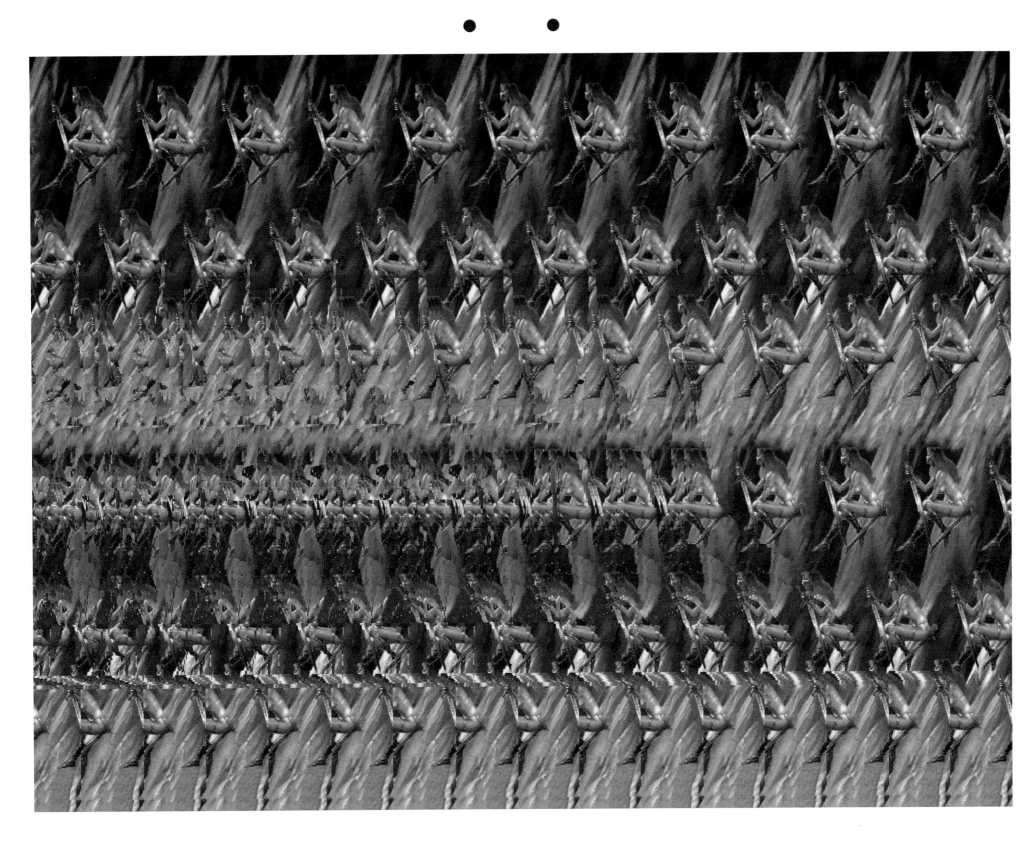

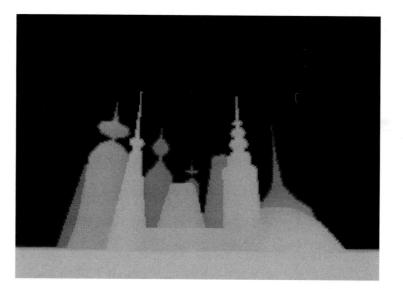

Samarkand

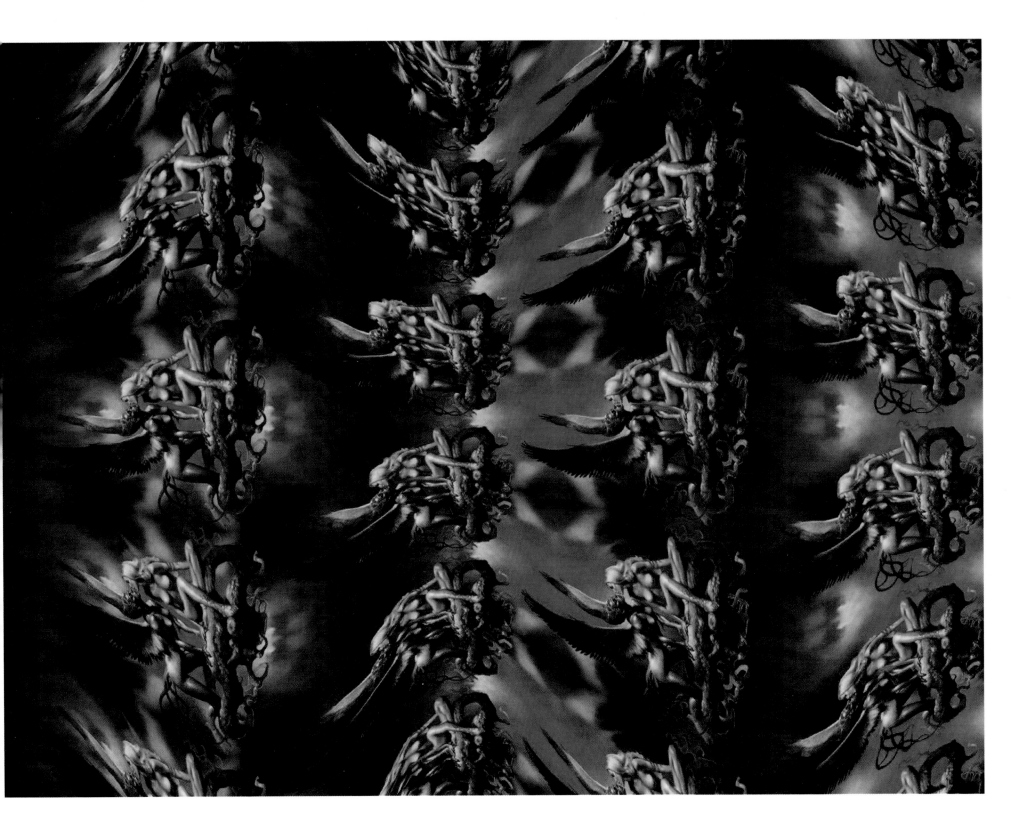

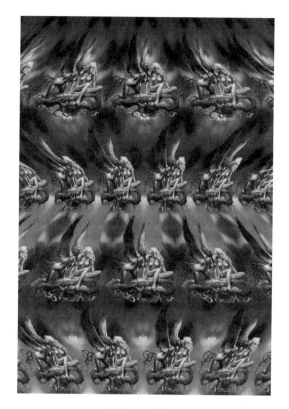

WAVE FORM

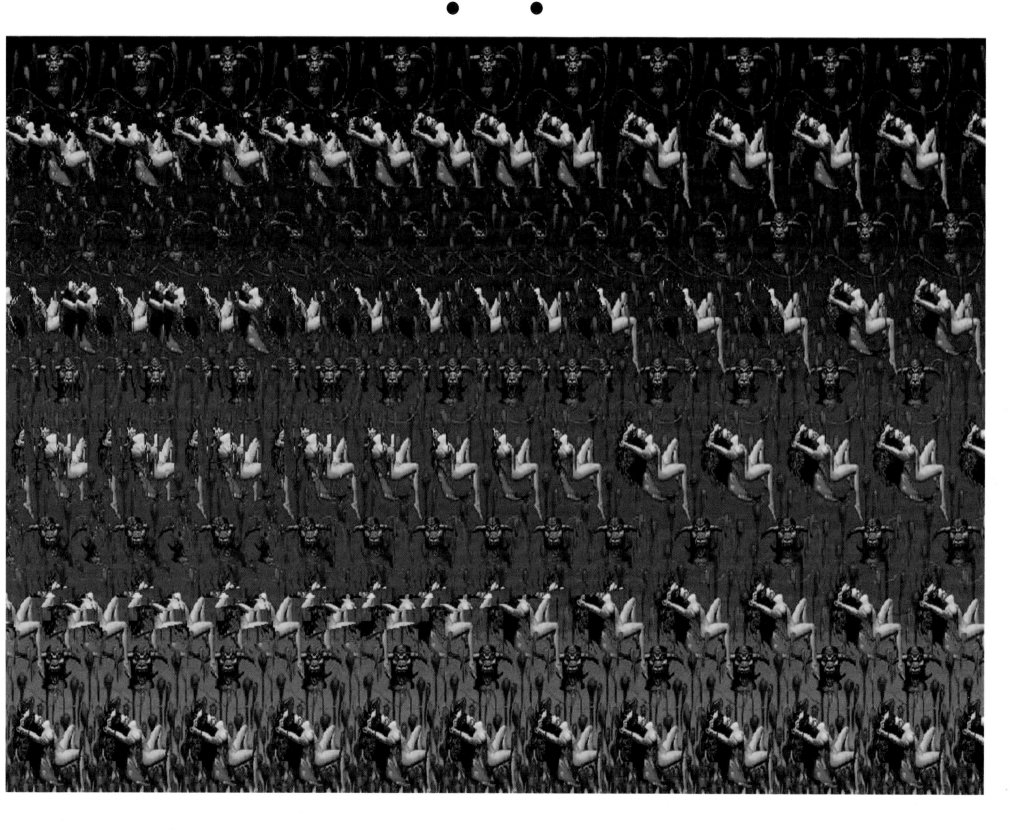

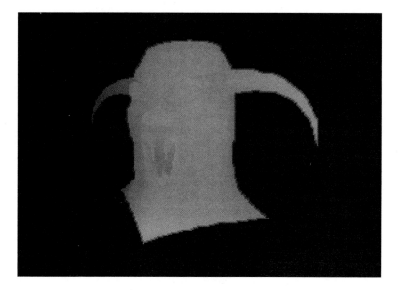

DEMONTED

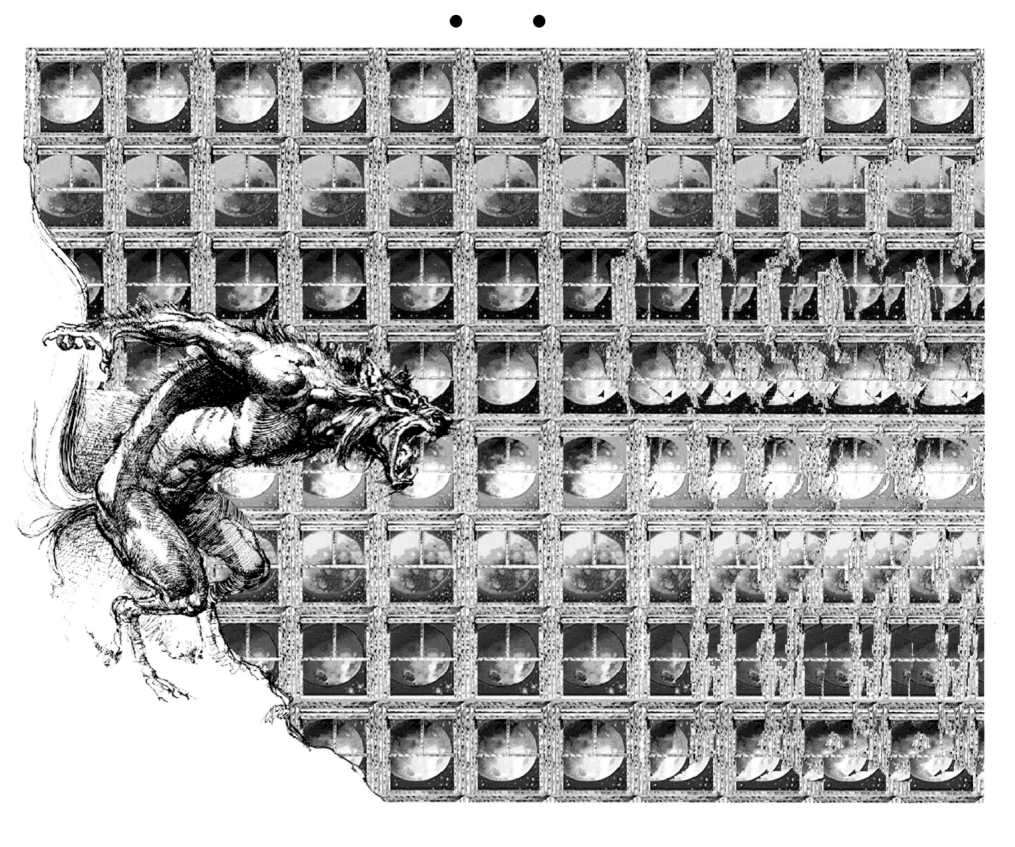

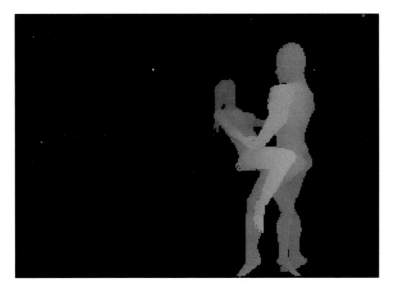

FULL MOON

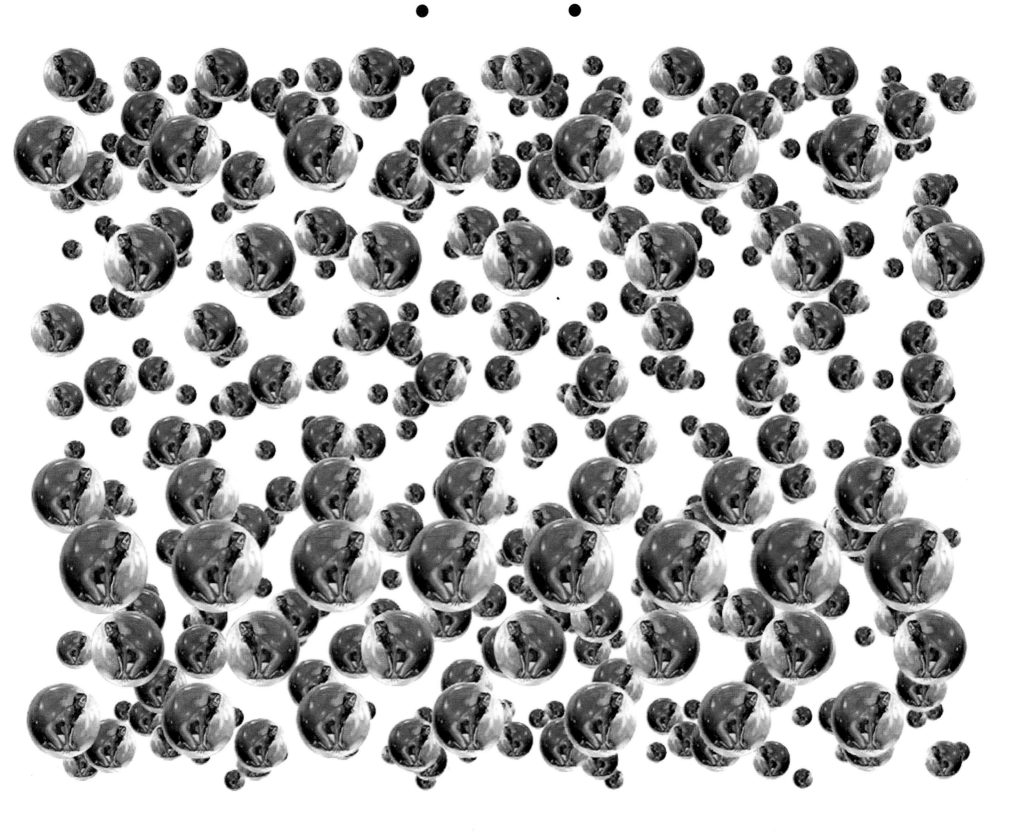

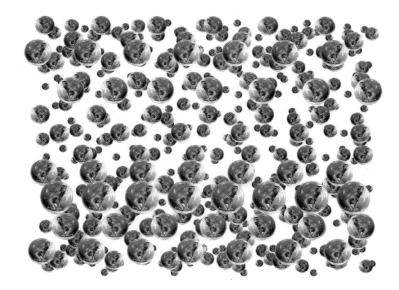

BUBBLE BATH

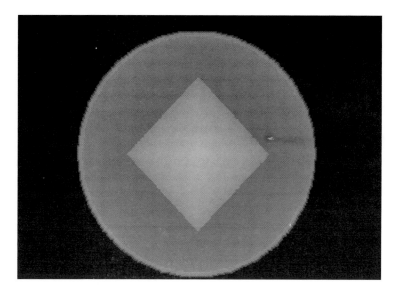

CRYSTAL GAZER

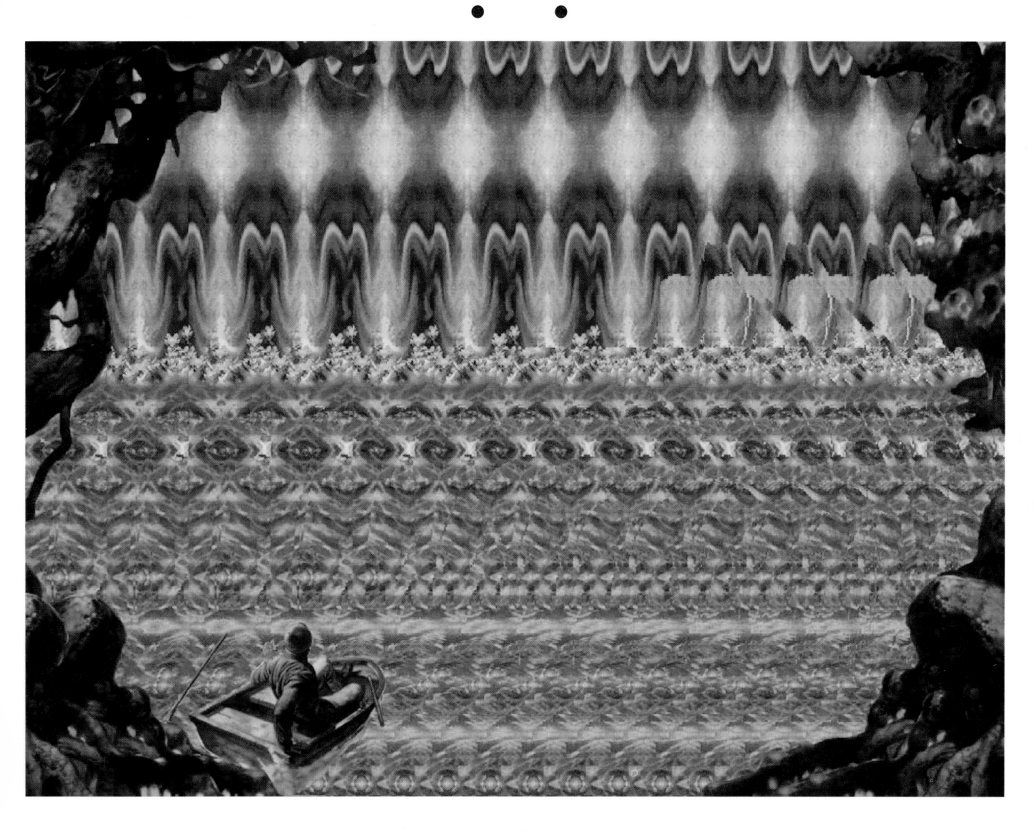

SWAMP THING

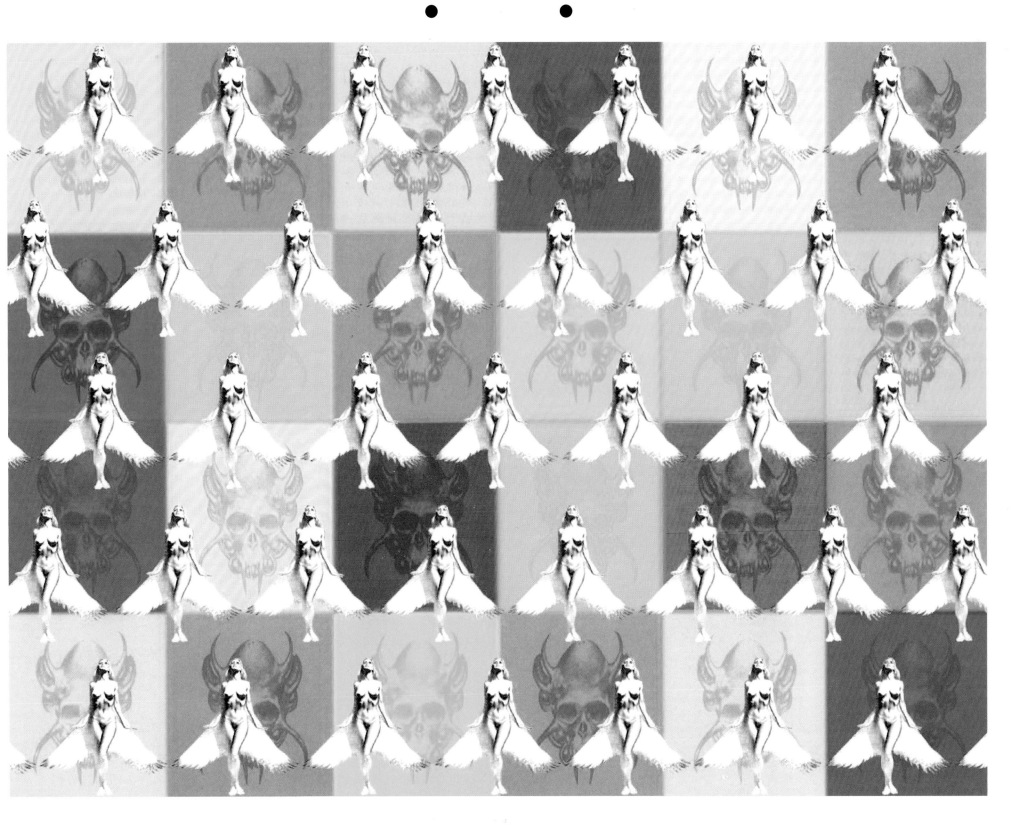

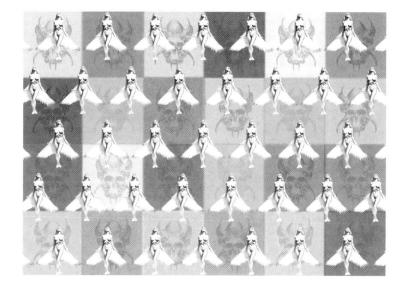

WARHOL'S ANGELS

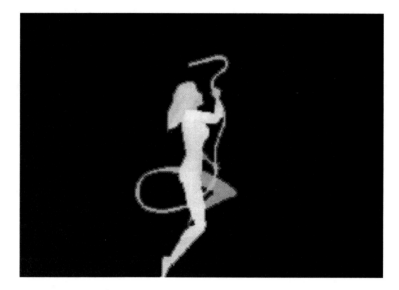

EAGLE'S KISS

MUSES

EVIL EYE

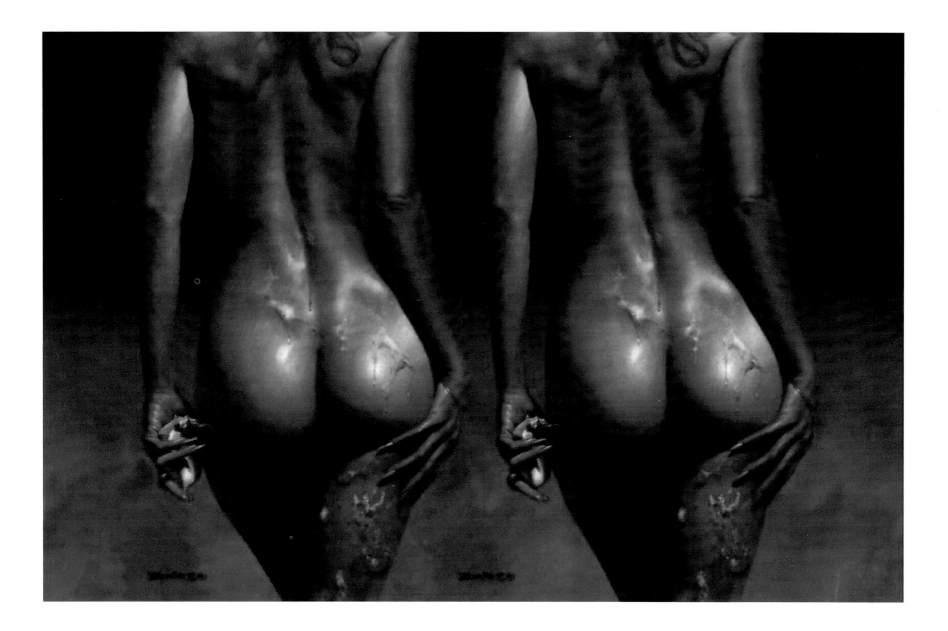

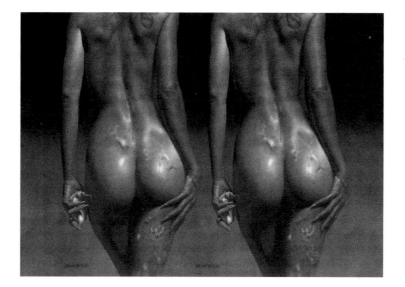

SOFT TOUCH

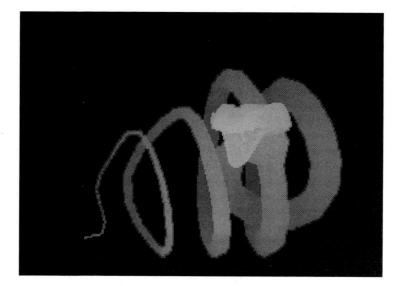

Medusa

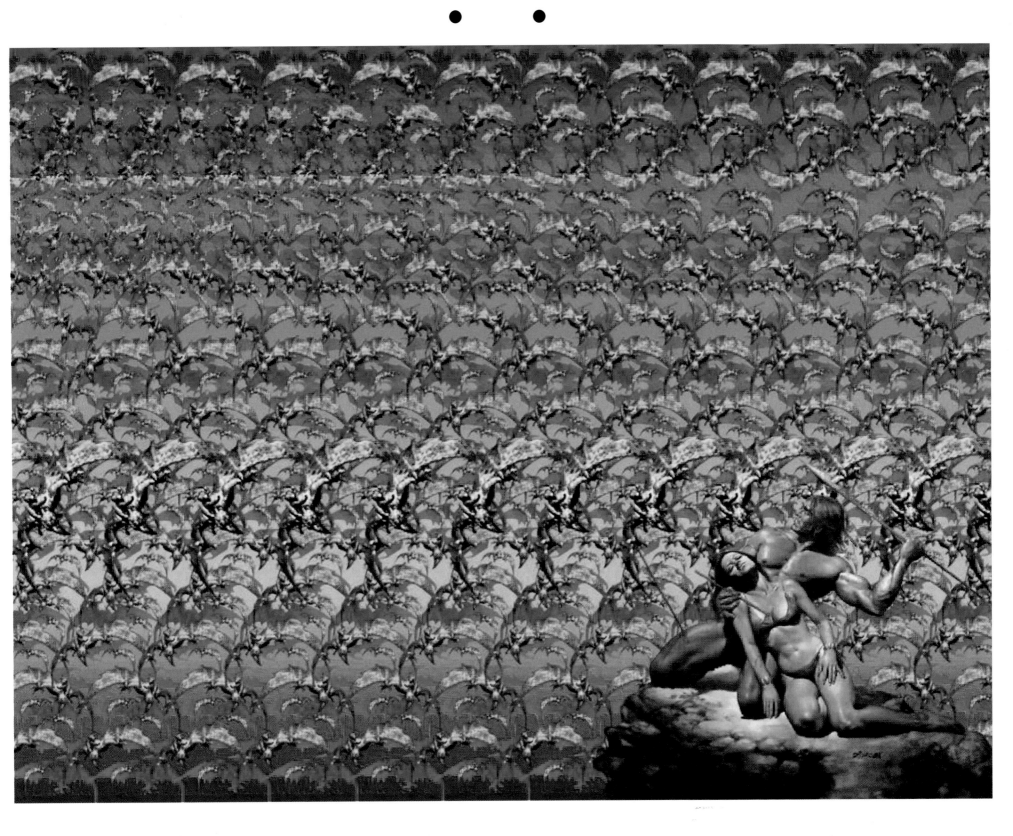

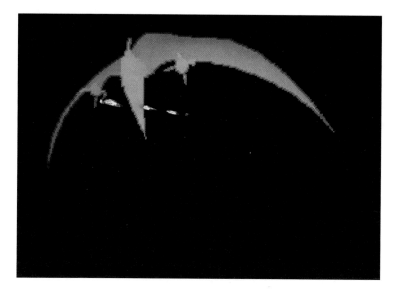

DRAGON RIDERS

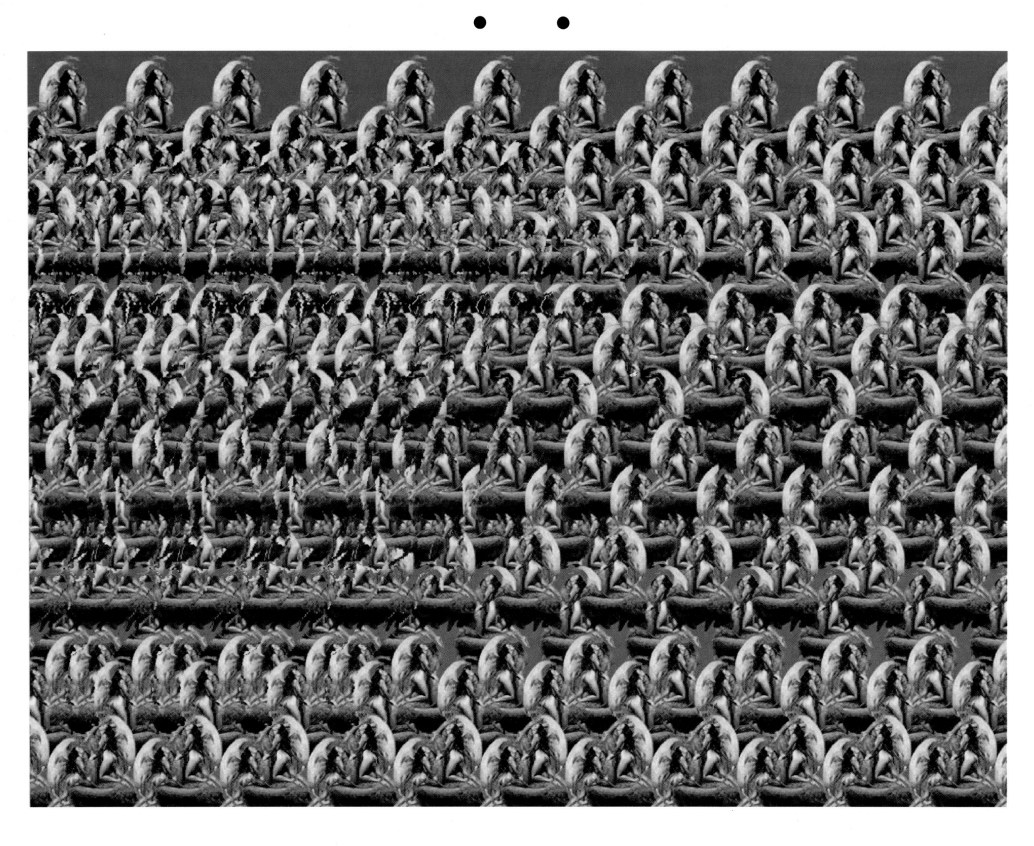

GUARDIAN ANGEL

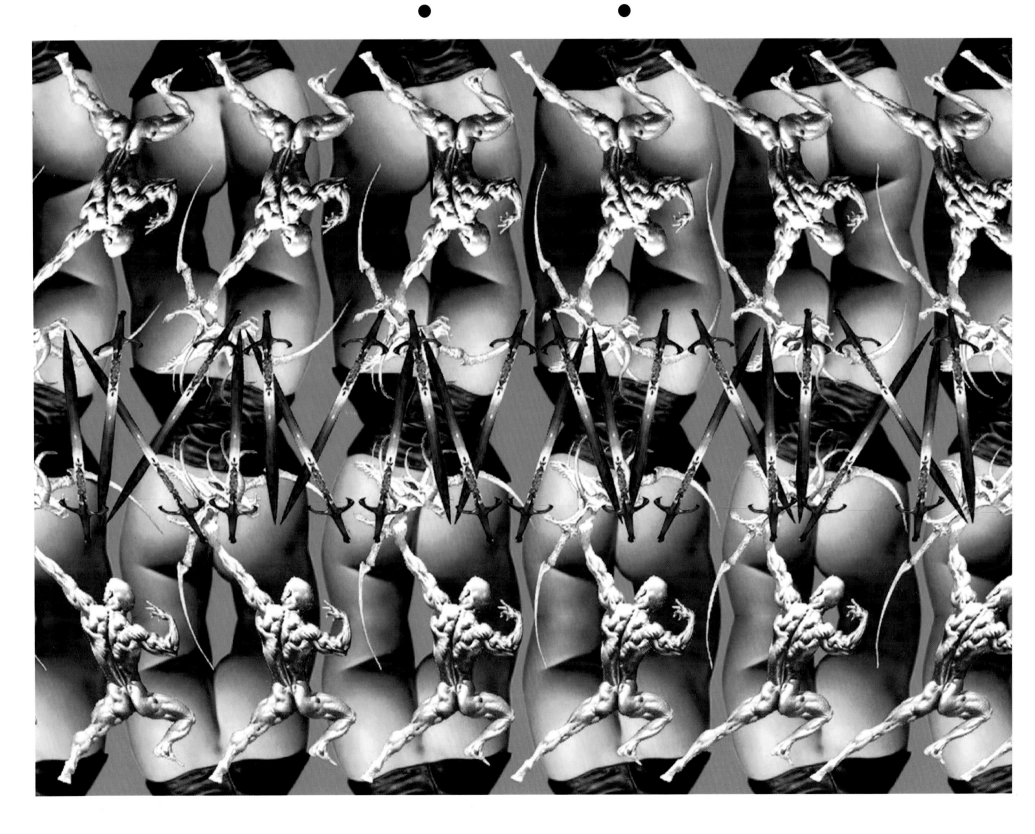

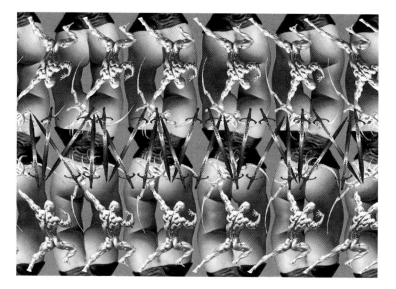

SURESHOT